"The Quotable" Cat

A Collection of Quotes, Facts and Lore for Feline Fanciers

Comp...

C.E. Cr...

HYSTERIA®
A DIVISION OF SOURCEBOOKS, INC.®
NAPERVILLE, ILLINOIS

Published by Sourcebooks, Inc.
P.O. Box 4410, Naperville, Illinois 60567-4410
(630) 961-3900
FAX: (630) 961-2168

Library of Congress Cataloging-in-Publication Data

Crimmins, C.E.
    The quotable cat : a collection of quotes, facts and lore for feline
fanciers / C.E. Crimmins
      p. cm.
    ISBN 1-887166-73-4 (alk. paper)
    1. Cats—Quotations, maxims, etc. 2. Cats—Miscellanea. I. Title.
PN6084.C23 Q67 2001
599.74'428—dc21

                                                    00-041982

        Printed and bound in the United States of America

          BG   10   9   8   7   6   5   4   3   2   1

For favorite felines, Cosmo, Lemon Leo, and Daisy. And for our dear departed, Felix, Boo-Boo, Shlomo, Lucille, Angie, Willie, Midgie, and Minnie. And, for two human favorites, Kelly and Alan, the man who cleans the kitty litter.

Contents

Acknowledgments

I would like to thank everyone who helped me to research and gather these quotes, including David Borgenicht, Steve Zorn, Nancy Steele, Tom Maeder, Jon Winokur, Bruce Schimmel, and Cindy Gitter. I especially want to thank Anne Kaier, who allowed me to include her delightful fable, "How Cats Came to Purr." Finally, I'm grateful to Deb Werksman for deciding to give the book another life. Seven more to go?

Introduction

When it comes to cats, geography is destiny. I grew up in the country, where our big red barn served as a beacon for cat-dumpers wanting to feel better about themselves ("Look—let's leave him near this farm. He can drink milk and eat mice.") Scores of cats passed through our property, where I learned firsthand Darwin's theory of natural selection. All my gorgeous gray favorites tangled unsuccessfully with automobiles—only kitties with enough white in their coats to be seen by headlights survived.

For years now I've lived in the middle of the city, another environment where cats just happen to you. Our tiny backyard is a well-known haven for unwed feline mothers, runaway kittens, and rakish toms. The idea of actually buying a cat has always seemed like paying for air to breathe.

Living with wall-to-wall hairball machines has its drawbacks, but I can't imagine residing anywhere without at least one feline companion. Ailurophilia—love of cats—is a congenital weakness of writers. Perhaps we admire an animal who appears even lazier to the general public than we do. On those days when lack of inspiration finds me staring off into space, I can always gain comfort from my dozing brood, one of whom is surely writing the Great Feline Novel while working hard to stay unconscious.

Are words adequate to describe those mysterious bundles of fur who sometimes deign to share our roofs? Over the centuries, mere human writers and thinkers have done surprisingly well in capturing the elusive pleasures of cat owning. I felt more than just a pang of recognition as I collected these words. I felt once again connected to the parade of wonderful beasts who have raised and lowered my blood pressure over the years and kept me from going stark raving mad in the lonely hours spent in front of a word processor.

My own cats tried to add interesting quotes by traipsing across the keyboard now and then, but I decided that the book would benefit more from their unseen presence. After all, no prose can measure up to the sheer delight of a cat fast asleep in one's lap.

C. C.
Philadelphia, Pennsylvania

The Quintessential Cat

A cat is a cat.

Spanish proverb

There are no ordinary cats.

Colette

There is some truth to the assertion that the cat, with the exception of a few luxury breeds…is no domestic animal but a completely wild being.

Konrad Lorenz

CAT: A pygmy lion who loves mice, hates dogs, and patronizes human beings.

Oliver Herford

A cat is never vulgar.

Carl Van Vechten

The really great thing about cats is their endless variety. One can pick a cat to fit almost any kind of decor, color scheme, income, personality, mood. But under the fur, whatever color it may be, there still lies, essentially unchanged, one of the world's free souls.

Eric Gurney

A god among creatures! Yet also a stray like me.

Tony Ross

Every cat is really the most beautiful woman in the room.

E. V. Lucas

Her function is to sit and be admired.

Georgina Strickland Gates

With their qualities of cleanliness, discretion, affection, patience, dignity, and courage, how many of us, I ask you, would be capable of being cats?

Fernand Mery

The cat is a dilettante in fur.

Theophile Gautier

A cat is a four-footed allergen.

Thomas Maeder

The cat of the slums and alleys, starved, outcast, harried, still keeps amid the prowlings of its adversity the bold, free, panther-tread with which it paced of yore the temple courts of Thebes, still displays the self-reliant watchfulness which man has never taught it to lay aside.

Saki (H. H. Munro)

The cat is witty, he has nerve, he knows how to do precisely the right thing at the right moment. He is impulsive and facetious and appreciates the value of a well-turned pleasantry. He extricates himself from the most difficult situations by a little pirouette. To how many timid and hesitating persons could he give useful lessons. I have never seen him embarassed. With an astounding promptitude he chooses instantly between two solutions of a problem, not merely that which is better from his point of view and in conformity with his interests, but also that which is elegant and gracious.

M. Poincaré

Cats are intended to teach us that not everything in nature has a function.

Garrison Keillor

And let me touch those curving claws of yellow ivory, and grasp the tail that like a monstrous asp coils round your heavy velvet paws.

Oscar Wilde

It is a crafty, subtle, watchful Creature, very loving and familiar with Mankind; but the mortal enemy of the Rat, Mouse, and every sort of Bird, which it seizes on as its Prey. Its flesh is not generally eaten, yet in some Countries is esteemed an excellent dish.

Maister Salmon

The cat enjoys a very special status as a domestic animal. There has been little artificial selection by man in cats, and many cats are allowed complete freedom of movement. In many respects the cats' way of life more closely resembles that of certain "wild" symbionts of man, like the rat or the house sparrow, than that of the true domestic, such as the dog.

Olof Liberg and Mikael Sandell

If man could be crossed with the cat, it would improve man but deteriorate the cat.

Mark Twain

They're the most graceful, sinuous, sexy, truly sensuous creatures in the world.

Carol Lawrence

A dog is a dog, a bird is a bird, and a cat is a person.

Mugsy Peabody

Cats are not people. It's important to stress that, because excessive cat watching often leads to the delusion that cats are people.

Dan Greenburg

For push of nose, for perseverance, there is nothing to beat a cat.

Emily Carr

One cat just leads to another.

Ernest Hemingway

Of all domestic animals the cat is the most expressive. His face is capable of showing a wide range of expressions. His tail is a mirror of his mind. His gracefulness is surpassed only by his agility. And, along with all these, he has a sense of humor.

Walter Chandoha

It is with the approach of winter that cats become in an especial manner our friends and guests. They sit in our chimney-corners, watch with us the dancing flames, and dream with us vague dreams, misty and melancholy as the deepening dusk.

Pierre Loti

Nominative, cat. Vocative, Puss.

Archbishop Whately

Amazing products, cats. And real simple to manufacture.

Michael O'Donoghue

I value in the cat the independent and almost ungrateful spirit which prevents her from attaching herself to any one, the indifference with which she passes from the salon to the housetop. When we caress her, she stretches herself, and arches her back responsively; but that is because she feels an agreeable sensation, not because she takes a silly satisfaction, like the dog, in faithfully loving a thankless master. The cat lives alone, has no need of society, obeys only when she pleases, pretends to sleep that she may see the more clearly, and scratches everything on which she can lay her paw.

Chateaubriand

There is not a man living who knows better than I that the four charms of a cat lie in its closed eyes, its long and lovely hair, its silence, and even its affected love.

Hilaire Belloc

For he has the subtlety and hissing of a serpent, which in goodness he suppresses.

Christopher Smart

The smallest feline is a masterpiece.

Leonardo Da Vinci

Cats, like men, are flatterers.

Wiliam S. Landor

Night and day, in gentleness or cruelty, for better or for worse, no other animal is as much of an extremist as the cat.

Fernand Mery

The cat is, above all things, a dramatist.

Margaret Benson

A cat is nobody's fool.

Heywood Broun

The phrase "domestic cat" is an oxymoron.

George Will

Cat People

Ernest Hemingway shared his Key West home with more than thirty cats.

Florence Nightingale owned more than sixty cats in her lifetime and often complained of mysterious "stains" on her paperwork.

Cardinal Richelieu, who had dozens of cats, built a "cattery" at Versailles in which to house them.

Mark Twain kept eleven cats at his farm in Connecticut. His daughter, Susy, once remarked, "The difference between Papa and Mamma is, that Mamma loves morals, and Papa loves cats."

Cat Lovers
and Their Pets

H. G. Wells — "Mr. Peter Wells"

Edgar Allan Poe — "Catarina"

Theodore Roosevelt — "Tom Quartz" and "Slippers"

Montaigne — "Madame Vanité"

Sir Walter Scott — "Hinse"

Jeremy Bentham — "Reverend Doctor John Langbourne"

Samuel Johnson — "Hodge"

Victor Hugo — "Chanoine" and "Gavroche"

Horace Walpole — "Selima"

Pope Leo XII (1760 - 1829) — "Micetto"

Raymond Chandler — "Taki"

Colette — "La Chat Dernier"

Mark Twain (Samuel Clemens) — "Blatherskite," "Sour Mash," "Stray Kit," "Sin," and "Satan"

Cats and Their Owners

Some men are born to cats, others have cats thrust upon them.

Gilbert Millstein

There is no evidence that at any time during its history the cat's way of life and its reception into human homesteads were purposely planned and directed by humans, as was the case with all other domestic animals at least from a very early stage of their association....In other words, there was no agent domesticating the cat besides the cat himself.

Paul Leyhausen

As every cat owner knows, nobody owns a cat.

Ellen Perry Berkeley

I love cats because I enjoy my home; and little by little, they become its visible soul.

Jean Cocteau

Cats are absolute individuals, with their own ideas about everything, including the people they own.

John Dingman

When a Cat adopts you there is nothing to be done about it except to put up with it and wait until the wind changes.

T. S. Eliot

Cats know how to obtain food without labor, shelter without confinement, and love without penalties.

W. L. George

Most cats have trained their owners. When the cat meows before the refrigerator, the owner obediently opens the door and feeds the cat. When it meows at the back door, the owner is trained to let the cat out.

Leon F. Whitney

Cats always know whether people like or dislike them. They do not always care enough to do anything about it.

Winifred Carriere

In his castle
He is king
And I his vassal...

Mildred R. Howland

A house without a cat, and a well-fed, well-petted, and properly revered cat, may be a perfect house, perhaps, but how can it prove its title?

Mark Twain

The majority of cat people, deep down, have a sneaking and half-recognized suspicion that they have been taken over by their feline, four-footed friend and that to a considerable extent she has imposed her whims and wishes upon the household.

Paul Gallico

An anthropomorphic view of the cat is very common among owners, but this fosters misunderstanding. A cat should always be seen as a cat, not as a human being.

Claudia Mertens and Rosemarie Schar

Two cats can live as cheaply as one, and their owner has twice as much fun.

Lloyd Alexander

Living with a cat is like being married to a career woman who can take domesticity or let it alone, so you'd better be nice to her.

Margaret Cooper Gay

It seems to me that the more useless a cat is the more he has earned his right to companionship. There are enough people "trying to make themselves useful" in this world without the added competition of cats.

Carl Van Vechten

Sometimes the veil between human and animal intelligence wears very thin—then one experiences the supreme thrill of keeping a cat, or perhaps allowing oneself to be owned by a cat.

Catherine Manley

People who lack self-confidence find it difficult, even impossible, to relate to a shy or timid cat. In this situation the cat's inclination to hide triggers feelings of rejection in the insecure person and the problem can easily escalate to the point where the person gives up the cat. Nurturant people, however, provide good homes for timid or even fearful cats.

Eileen B. Karsh and Dennis C. Turner

The way to keep a cat is to try to chase it away.

E. W. Howe

One cannot woo a cat after the fashion of the Conqueror. Courtesy, tact, patience, are needed at every step.

Agnes Repplier

A woman and a cat. Mention the two in the same breath and most men's eyes roll skyward. They know all about that combination. Spinsters, they note, have many cats. So do crazy ladies. A lot of my single friends share their hearths with two or more furry friends. Among us, there is some wackiness, but it's not pronounced. I doubt that any one of us will make the headlines: "Old Maid Leaves Estate to Three Hundred Cats."

For the record, we all like men just as much as we like kittens. We even recognize that in certain situations, men are far superior. But while we'll accept baldness, bad table manners, even temporary sexual dysfunction, negative vibes towards cats get a new man quickly crossed off our list.

Cathryn Jakobson

Cats are dangerous companions for writers because cat watching is a near-perfect method of writing avoidance.

Dan Greenburg

It is, of course, totally pointless to call a cat when it is intent on the chase. They are deaf to the interruptive nonsense of humans. They are on cat business, totally serious and involved.

John D. MacDonald

Cats, like women, should be respected as individuals rather than admired as decoration, but there's no harm, given a choice, in taking up with a strikingly attractive specimen of either.

Barbara Holland

To a cat, human beings are an inferior, servile race, always to be kept in their places, with occasional rewards if they perform well. To love a cat is uphill work, and therefore very rewarding.

Haskel Frankel

Getting a cat is a greater commitment than getting married.

Seymour and Paula Chwast

This switch from tame pet to wild animal and then back again is fascinating to watch. Any cat owner who has accidentally come across the pet cat when it is deeply involved in some feline soap opera of sex and violence will know what I mean. One instant the animal is totally wrapped up in an intense drama of courtship or status. Then out of the corner of its eye it spots its human owner watching the proceedings. There is a schizoid moment of double involvement, a hesitation, and the animal runs across, rubs against its owner's leg, and becomes the house kitten once more.

Desmond Morris

Karsh and Burket asked all their prospective owners to rate themselves on scales of loneliness, anxiety, and depression before adopting a cat and several times afterwards. At year's end, the long-term owners felt less lonely, less anxious, and less depressed. Although the owners and non-owners did not differ initially in loneliness, anxiety, and depression, they did differ significantly by the end of one year.

Karsh and Burket also found evidence of physiological benefits. Four of the elderly cat owners had high blood pressure before the adoption and two were also diabetic. All four showed reduced blood pressure that has been maintained for over two years.

Ownership study reported in *Domestic Feline Behavior*

Throughout the Midi of France people believe in "matagots" or magician-cats. They are black and have the power to attract wealth to the house where they are well fed and cared for. To catch a matagot you must lure it with a chicken and then grab it by the tail and carry it home in a sack without once looking backwards. Having got your matagot home, put it in a chest and always give it the first mouthful every time you eat. This will ensure that every morning you will find a gold coin at the bottom of the chest.

Mildred Kirk

Wanted, by a lady of rank, for adequate remuneration, a few well-behaved and respectably dressed children, to amuse a cat in delicate health two or three hours a day.

Late nineteenth century ad in Berlin newspaper

Cats, even when robust, have scant liking for the boisterous society of children, and are apt to exert their utmost ingenuity to escape it.

Agnes Repplier

If we have a decent sort of cat to begin with, and have always treated it courteously, and aren't cursed with meddling, bullying natures, it's a pleasure to let it do as it pleases. With children, this would be wicked and irresponsible, so raising children involves a lot of effort and friction. They need to be taught how to tie their shoes and multiply fractions, they need to be punished for pocketing candy in the grocery store, they need to be washed and combed and forced to clean up their rooms and say please and thank you.

A cat is our relief and our reward.

Barbara Holland

Saintly Cats

Although cats often symbolized Satan in early Christian stories, a number of saints flouted tradition by keeping feline companions:

St. Agatha is still known as Santo Gato (Saint Cat) in parts of the Pyrenees mountains of southwestern France. She is said to appear in the form of a cat on her day, February 5, to punish women who have angered her.

St. Jerome was famous for owning a cat, and is frequently depicted in paintings with a domestic cat instead of his more traditional lion mascot.

St. Francis of Assisi, according to one Italian legend, was saved from a plague of mice by a cat which sprang miraculously out of his sleeve.

St. Gregory the Great possessed no worldly goods except a cat, which he liked to stroke and hold in his arms while he was meditating.

St. Molig of Ireland, according to one story, became disturbed when his pet cat caught a sparrow which had eaten a fly; he restored both bird and insect to life.

St. Ives, the patron saint of lawyers, appears in portraits with a cat by his side, or is sometimes depicted as a cat.

Catnip of the Gods

In Ancient Egypt they were worshipped as gods. This makes them too prone to set themselves up as critics of the frail and erring human beings whose lot they share.

P. G. Wodehouse

Cats have always inspired mystical reveries. A brief list of the feline's association with deities:

* *Bast*, Egyptian Fertility Goddess, was often represented by a cat and worshipped in a vast cult in Egypt from 1780 B.C. until A.D. 392. One version of her name, "Pasht" might have given rise to the English term "puss."

* *Ra*, Egyptian Sun God (also known as Osiris), often changed himself into a cat to do battle with the serpent-like darkness.

* *Diana*, Greek Goddess of Wisdom, was represented by the moon, a potent cat symbol (hunter of the night) throughout the ages.

* *Two gray cats* drew the chariot of Freya, Scandinavian Goddess of Love and Beauty. The kitties also played around her ankles as a symbol of her domesticity.

* *Tsun-Kyanske*, the Burmese Goddess of the Trans-mutation of Souls, was attended by priests and their cats, animals reportedly able to communicate directly with the goddess.

* *The Babylonian Gods* of Silver, Gold, and Wood were depicted with cats sitting on their shoulders.

* *Siamese (Thai) Kings*, believed godlike, required a cat for their souls to pass into upon death, so that the soul could rest for the cat's natural life span before entering Paradise.

* *Malaysians* venerated the cat as a godlike creature who eased their afterlife journey from Hell to Paradise. Anyone who killed a cat was required to carry and stack as many coconut tree trunks as the cat had hairs.

The Mind
of a Cat

We cannot, without becoming cats, perfectly understand the cat mind.

St. George Mivart

To understand a cat, you must realize that he has his own gifts, his own viewpoint, even his own morality.

Lillian Jackson Braun

Way down deep, we're all motivated by the same urges. Cats have the courage to live by them.

Jim Davis

The smart cat doesn't let on that he is.

H. G. Frommer

Cats seldom make mistakes and they never make the same mistake twice.

Carl Van Vechten

Unlike us, cats never outgrow their delight in cat capacities, nor do they settle finally for limitations. Cats, I think, live out their lives fulfilling their expectations.

Irving Townsend

As it crosses the threshold the cat becomes transformed. The kitten-of-man brain is switched off and the wild-cat brain is clicked on....The cat's mind has floated off into another, totally feline world, where strange bipedal apes have no place.

Desmond Morris

I can see him now, standing on the sill, looking about the sky as if he was thinking whether it were worthwhile to take an umbrella.

Charles Dudley Warner

Cats virtually always underestimate human intelligence just as we, perhaps, underestimate theirs.

Roger Caras

The cat has too much spirit to have no heart.

Ernest Menault

The little furry buggers are just deep, deep wells you throw all your emotions into.

Bruce Schimmel

It's tough to judge cats. Here we are with our three-pound brains and a hundred billion neurons packed into our skulls, trying to figure out a critter with a one- to two-ounce brain and perhaps ten billion neurons.

Penny Ward Moser

Of all animals, he alone attains the Contemplative Life. He regards the wheel of existence from without, like the Buddha.

Andrew Lang

Cats do things that are very human. I don't make a great distinction between human and cat intelligence—it seems to be a question of degree rather than of kind.

Jean Holtzworth, D.V.M.

It always gives me a shiver when I see a cat seeing what I can't see.

Eleanor Farjeon

Who can believe that there is no soul behind those luminous eyes!

Theophile Gautier

In laboratory testing, cats are the only species aside from primates in which learning by observation has been demonstrated. In tasks such as pulling on a string or pressing a lever to release a latch on a door, cats allowed to watch others learn these tasks learned the same tasks themselves much more rapidly than the naive learners.

Benjamin L. Hart, D.V. M.

Cat memory is a funny thing. We have a roll-over cat. It's the one we send whenever anybody needs a cat to roll over. It's a smart cat, and knows other tricks. But whenever it gets stressed out on the set it just keeps rolling over.

Anonymous Hollywood animal trainer

Cats are a mysterious kind of folk. There is more passing in their minds than we are aware of.

Sir Walter Scott

I wonder what goes through his mind when he sees us peeing in his water bowl.

Penny Ward Moser

The Quotable Cat

My cat never laughs or cries; he is always reasoning.

Unamuno

As to sagacity, I should say that his judgment respecting the warmest place and the softest cushion in a room is infallible, his punctuality at meal times is admirable, and his pertinacity in jumping on people's shoulders till they give him some of the best of what is going, indicates great firmness.

Thomas Henry Huxley

It is remarkable, in cats, that the outer life they reveal to their masters is one of perpetual confident boredom.

Robley Wilson, Jr.

I have studied many philosophers and many cats. The wisdom of cats is infinitely superior.

Hippolyte Taine

If a cat does something, we call it instinct; if we do the same thing, for the same reason, we call it intelligence.

Will Cuppy

The cat seldom interferes with other people's rights. His intelligence keeps him from doing many of the fool things that complicate life.

Carl Van Vechten

The cat, like the genius, draws into itself as into a shell except in the atmosphere of congeniality, and this is the secret of its remarkable and elusive personality.

Ida M. Mellen

I respect cats, they seem to have so much else in their heads besides their mess.

Ralph Waldo Emerson

A man has to work so hard so that something of his personality stays alive. A tomcat has it so easy, he has only to spray and his presence is there for years on a rainy day.

Albert Einstein

If you want to be a psychological novelist and write about human beings, the best thing you can do is keep a pair of cats.

Aldous Huxley

One Way to Hypnotize a Cat

In 1914, Professor Mangold of the University of Fribourg, Switzerland, hypnotized hundreds of semi-wild, nasty tomcats. Here, according to French historian Fernand Mery, is the technique:

"This method consists of taking hold of the cat with a rapid movement and laying it quickly down on its side or its back. As soon as its first defensive reflexes are calmed, a kind of rocking movement or alternating rotation is imposed on the complete body until, after a shorter or longer time, the subject, far from reacting, abandons itself completely and little by little becomes completely immobile."

The Language of Cats

In my house you have to talk to cats because, being ten of them, there are a lot of important things you have to say to them—like "Get off" and "Shut up" and things like that.

Beryl Reid

Cats have a contempt of speech. Why should they talk when they can communicate without words?

Lilian Jackson Braun

Cats do not declare their love much; they enact it, by their myriad invocations of our pleasure.

Vicki Hearne

He was sitting in front of the door. It is a known fact that if one sits long enough in front of a door, doing the proper yoga exercises, the door will open.

May Sarton

The cat's large variety of facial expressions is not equaled by those of any other animal save man.

Ida M. Mellen

When Minnie wants my attention, she performs a strange dipping motion with her head that makes her look like Katharine Hepburn.

C. E. Crimmins

His advances were subtle: a movement of his head, a light grazing of our legs with his flank, a glance, a moment of purring. Unobvious things that we gradually learned to observe and interpret. The nearest Rabbit came to effusiveness was rolling—his specialty. He would sink down in a long, slow glide until his head touched the floor, then deftly throw himself over on his back, wiggling his hind paws in a supreme gesture of good will. But a cat usually writes his love notes in shorthand and reading them demands a certain amount of practice.

Lloyd Alexander

Meow is like aloha—it can mean anything.

Hank Ketchum

Feline communicators divide naturally into two groups: acrobatic types who hang on the screen door when they want to come in, and the verbalizers who use yowling as a calling card.

Leo Dworken

When your cat rubs the side of its face along your leg, it's affectionately marking you with its scent, identifying you as its private property, saying, in effect, "You belong to me."

Susan McDonough, D.V.M.

A cat is there when you call her—if she doesn't have something better to do.

Bill Adler

She claws at the window, meows and looks beseechingly at me where I sit reading. When I come to the window she no longer meows with sound. Only the mouth opens in a silent imploring prayer.

Liv Ullman

Most people talk to their cats the way they'd talk to the coffee grinder.

Ian Dunbar

Cats, especially, have a finely tuned sense of an ESP, non-verbal language that allows them to sort out situations in their minds long before we humans can. Believe it or not, this non-verbal communication is not limited by space or time. You can communicate with your cat while sitting at the office. You can pick up his or her feelings of loneliness when you have developed the listening skills that are innate to your feline.

Beatrice Lydecker

There's this great jealousy: I sometimes have the terrible feeling that you do transfer your emotions to cats, and since I am myself a violently sexually jealous woman I think I passed it all on to the cats!

Eileen Atkins

The tail, in cats, is the principal organ of emotional expression, and a Manx cat is the equivalent of a dumb man.

Aldous Huxley

Slowly, with a look of intense concentration, he got up and advanced on me...put out a front paw, and stroked my cheek as I used to stroke his chops. A human caress from a cat. I felt very meagre and ill-educated that I could not purr.

Sylvia Townsend Warner

A cat kiss is a long, slow blink with your gaze and attention fixed on the cat's eyes before, during, and after the blink. When throwing a cat kiss, I always think the phrase "I love you." ("I" before, "love" during, and "you" after the blink.)

Anitra Frazier

Cats seem to go on the principle that it never does any harm to ask for what you want.

Joseph Wood Krutch

Licking is the cat's first and most fundamental method of communication because that's the first experience the new-born kitten has. It's usually reserved for other cats or the most important humans. If your cat licks you, you should be very flattered because this is a natural and sincere demonstration of the companionship bond it has for you.

Susan McDonough, D.V.M.

You opened the door for her if she crossed the room and gave you a look. She made you know what she meant as if she had the gift of speech.

Sarah Orne Jewett

There is no cat "language." Painful as it is for us to admit, they don't need one.

Barbara Holland

When I speak to her she can look the other way in an elaborate show of inattention, but those black ears are turning like radar scopes, taking in everything.

Betty White

Often he would sit looking at me, and then, moved by a delicate affection, come and pull my coat and sleeve until he could touch my face with his nose, and then go away contented.

Charles Dudley Warner

Cats can give you a round-eyed stare, they can narrow their eyes to slits and blink slowly with pleasure; they even have a way of flattening their upper lids in a straight horizontal line when they are insulted or perplexed. They can open their eyes wide with anxiety when they're imploring you to do something for them. Anger, even make-believe fury while playing, can widen the pupils so the eyes appear almost black.

Patricia Curtis

At dinner time he would sit in a corner, concentrating, and suddenly they would say, "Time to feed the cat," as if it were their own idea.

Lilian Jackson Braun

When a cat looks at you and then half closes its eyes, it's not ignoring you. The animal is telling you that it's relaxed in your presence. A scared cat would stare at you and hiss, or run away if you moved toward it. And you would see the pupils of its eyes dilate, a clear sign of fear.

Michael W. Fox, D.V.M.

My simple "Goodbye, I'll be back tonight" communication is transmitted with accompanying thoughts that go something like this: "We'll see-touch each other with gladness when it's black dark night outside the window." I picture and feel myself seeing and touching Purr. Then I add the emotion of gladness and picture the dark window in the background to give a time reference.

Later that night when it all comes true, it is always a sort of supernatural feeling as I mentally watch while Purr and I live out the picture I promised him that morning.

Anitra Frazier

I don't make any claims that cats have a language as we know it. They do have distinct vocalizations for different situations. "Meow," for instance, is usually reserved for humans. The "me" part is a greeting, like "Hi!" The "ow" part is aggressive. It says, "I have rights here, too."

Patricia McKinley

"**W**hat can that cat want?" I said to myself. "She has had her dinner. She is not hungry. What is she after?"

In answer to my unspoken question, la Chinoise crept nearer and nearer until she could touch my foot. Then, sitting upright, with her tail curled close about her, she uttered a gentle little cry, gazing meanwhile straight into my eyes which seemed to hold some message she could read. She understood that I was a thinking creature, capable of pity, and accessible to such mute and piteous prayer; and that my eyes were the mirrors in which her anxious little soul must study my good or bad intentions. It is terrifying to think how near an animal comes to us, when it is capable of such intercourse as this.

Pierre Loti

Once when she was in heat, I lost patience with her constant "come-and-get-me" yelling. In irritation, I found myself yelling back at her in exact imitation. This turned out to be just what the little witch wanted, and it delighted her beyond measure.

Winifred Carriere

The Idiomatic Cat

No room to swing a cat does not refer directly to cats, but to the nine-knotted cat-o'-nine-tails whip used to punish wayward sailors. The whip was too long to swing below deck, so punishment was always administered outdoors. The whip was often called a "cat" because the marks it left on a sailor's back looked like scratches.

Having kittens, a phrase that connotes severe anxiety, is a leftover from the days of witchcraft, when pregnant women experiencing long, painful labors were often said to be bewitched and about to give birth to a litter of felines.

Raining cats and dogs has two possible explanations. Years ago, cities had inadequate drainage, so after a torrential rainstorm people would emerge from their houses to find many dead cats and dogs on the streets. Or, the phrase could be a corruption of the Greek word for waterfall, catadupa, which, when repeated frequently, becomes "cats and dogs."

A Brief History of Felines

ca. 2,000 B.C. The Abyssinian becomes the first domestic cat to appear in a painting.

A.D. 511 – 528 King Childebert of France displays a royal crest depicting a cat.

ca. 800 An unknown Irish monk writes a poem praising his white cat, entitled "Pangur Ban." At about the same time, illustrations of cats appear in the margins of Irish religious manuscripts.

1205 The English Nun's Rule condones ownership: "Ye shall not possess any beast, my dear sisters, except only a cat."

ca. 1350 The manuscript, the *Cat Book Poems*, begins circulating in Thailand (the first of the cat book industry?).

1662 The famous Scottish witch, Isobel Gowdie, confesses at her trial that it is a common practice of her sisters to change themselves into cats and roam about at night. She is convicted and burned at the stake.

1669 In the Swedish village of Mohra, over three hundred children from six to sixteen years of age confess to being bewitched by Satan, who has given them each a cat that steals butter, cheese, milk, and bacon. The children claim they have taken their cats to parties at Satan's palace, "Blockula."

1750 Cats are officially introduced into the American colonies from England to help control the rodent population.

1760 An anonymous pamphlet, "The Life and Adventures of a Cat," introduces Tom the Cat, who becomes so popular that afterwards male cats are known as "tomcats" instead of "ram cats."

1789 A cat is used as a symbol of liberty in the French Revolution.

1797 A mysterious cat epidemic strikes Philadelphia, leaving hundreds of felines dead on doorsteps.

1868 London bureaucrats introduce the Cat System, whereby three cats receive a salary of two shillings per week to keep down the mouse population in public buildings.

1871 A journalist describes "an unnatural, nightmare kind of cat," introduced at the first national cat show at the Crystal Palace in London. The cat is a seal-point Siamese.

1888 A farmer digs up an ancient cat necropolis in Beni Hasan, Egypt, containing thousands of mummified cats. Present also are embalmed mice for afterworld snacking. Most of the remains end up being shipped to England and sold by the ton as fertilizer.

1910 Krazy Kat, the philosopher-cat cartoon starring the stylized Krazy and sidekick Ignatz Mouse is first drawn by George Herriman. The animated version follows in 1916.

1917 Thomas Kat, the prototype of Felix the Cat, is introduced by Pat Sullivan and Otto Messmer. In the 1920s, the Felix craze will spawn toys, books, games, and other artifacts.

1939 Poet T. S. Eliot publishes *Old Possum's Book of Practical Cats*, proving that even Nobel prizewinners can be hopelessly silly about felines.

1947 Ed Lowe invents kitty litter, opening the door for increased popularity of cats as house pets.

1950 A four-month-old kitten climbs the Matterhorn (10,820 feet) following a climbing party that set out from the Hotel Belvedere.

1970 *The Mary Tyler Moore Show* premieres, marking the debut of the famous MTM kitten logo parody of the MGM lion.

1973 California Governor Ronald Reagan signs a bill into state law that specifies prison penalties for kicking or injuring another person's cat.

1973 Morris the Cat, star of Nine Lives Cat Food commercials, wins the coveted Patsy, the animal kingdom's version of the Oscar.

1974 Ralph Bakshi creates the first X-rated animated film, *Fritz the Cat*, based on Robert Crumb's underground comic strip.

1975 Squeak, a Siamese cat, escapes from his carrier in the cargo hold of an airplane and ends up traveling 19,790 miles before airline personnel find him, unharmed.

1978 "Garfield" joins United Features Syndicate and makes creator Jim Davis a millionaire.

1982 The Broadway musical *Cats*, based on T. S. Eliot's book of cat poems and featuring Andrew Lloyd Weber's music, arrives in the U.S. from London to become one of the longest-running shows ever.

1987 Felines catapult over dogs to become the No. 1 pet in America, with fifty-six million cats in households across the country compared with fifty-two million canines.

1993 Chelsea Clinton's cat, Socks, moves into the White House and becomes First Feline.

1997 ABC's comedy *Sabrina, The Teenage Witch* premieres, making Salem the Cat a prime time television star.

The Celluloid Cat

A Selective Filmography

Bell, Book, and Candle (1959) A delightful comedy celebrating the connection between witches and cats. Starring Pyewacket the black cat and, in supporting roles, James Stewart, Kim Novak, Jack Lemmon, and Ernie Kovacs. Directed by Richard Quine, 106 minutes.

That Darn Cat! (1964) A feline hero stumbles across some criminals. This Disney film stars D.C. the Siamese cat and Homo sapiens Dean Jones, Hayley Mills, Dorothy Provine, Roddy McDowell, William Demarest, and Elsa Lanchester. Directed by Robert Stevenson, 116 minutes.

The Three Lives of Thomasina (1965) Sappy but cute tale in which a time-tripping tabby goes to kitty heaven and comes back to help a little girl. Two-legged supporting cast includes Patrick McGoohan, Susan Hampshire, Karen Dotrice, and Vincent Winter. Directed by Don Chaffey, ninety-seven minutes.

Harry and Tonto (1974) The first—and last—of its kind, a buddy road movie featuring an old guy and his cat. Tonto is wonderful, and so are furless actors Art Carney, Ellen Burstyn, and Larry Hagman. Directed by Paul Mazursky, 115 minutes.

The Cat from Outer Space (1978) About as silly as its title. Jake is a cat who, by virtue of the fact that he is from another planet, will probably remind owners of their own pets. He wears a collar with special powers and is not upstaged by humans Ken Berry, Sandy Duncan, and Harry Morgan. Directed by Norman Tokar, 103 minutes.

Cat and...Dog

Researchers have discovered that dogs can comprehend a vocabulary of two thousand words, whereas cats can only comprehend twenty-five to fifty. No one ever asks how many cat words researchers can comprehend.

Cats don't bark and act brave when they see something small in fur or feathers, they kill it. Dogs tend to bravado. They're braggarts. In the great evolutionary drama the dog is Sergeant Bilko, the cat is Rambo.

James Gorman

A cat has never been known to bite the garbageman.

H. Monger Burdock

As a pet, a dog is your good buddy, and he communicates with you. A cat is your good buddy too, but he just doesn't speak your language.

Peter Borchelt

The dog may be man's best friend, but it is rarely allowed out on its own to wander from garden to garden or street to street. The obedient dog has to be taken for a walk. The headstrong cat walks alone.

Desmond Morris

You can usually tell by looking at it what's going on inside a dog. Except for the few Thurberian neurotics, a dog wears his insides on his outside, writ large and plain. A cat thinks at the back of its head, and the results can surprise you. No wonder cats were burned as witches; it hurts people's feelings not to know what the lower orders are up to.

Barbara Holland

What is the difference between dog owners and cat owners?

A dog owner enters the aisle marked "Pet Supplies," grabs a twenty-five-pound sack and is on his way. Total elapsed time: two seconds.

A cat owner enters the aisle, pulls his cart out of the way, and stands in front of the cans. He thinks: "She wouldn't eat turkey with giblets last week. She clawed the wall in disgust when I gave her mixed grill. And she doesn't seem to like chicken with liver gravy anymore." Nearing despair as other cat-owning shoppers begin to crowd him, he carefully chooses ten new and different flavors. Total elapsed time: five minutes.

Kathleen Fury

A dog is like a liberal. He wants to please everybody. A cat really doesn't need to know that everybody loves him.

William Kunstler

Subtle, the opposite of dogs,
And, unlike dogs, capable
Of flirting, falling, and yawning anywhere...

Louis MacNeice

If I tell my dog, "Come here," he runs right over with a "Yes, what can I do for you?" look. The cat's response is "Put it in writing, and I'll get back to you."

Anonymous

To respect the cat is the beginning of the aesthetic sense. At a stage of culture when utility governs all of its judgments, mankind prefers the dog.

Erasmus Darwin

Your cat will never threaten your popularity by barking at three in the morning. He won't attack the mailman or eat the drapes, although he may climb the drapes to see how the room looks from the ceiling.

Helen Powers

Why, I wonder, should a great many good men and women cherish an unreasonable grudge against one animal because it does not chance to possess the precise qualities of another? "My dog fetches my slippers for me every night," said a friend trimphantly, not long ago. "He puts them first to warm by the fire, and then brings them over to my chair, wagging his tail, and as proud as Punch. Would your cat do as much for you, I'd like to know?" Assuredly not! If I waited for Agrippina to fetch me shoes or slippers, I should have not other recourse but to join as speedily as possible one of the barefooted religious orders of Italy.

Agnes Repplier

If animals could speak as fabulists have feigned, the dog would be a blunt, outspoken, honest fellow, but the cat would have the rare talent of never saying a word too much.

Carl Van Vechten

Dogs instinctively realize that cats are smarter than they are, so they resent the intrusion of a cat upon the household.

Eric Gurney

A cat is a demure animal; it will not come into the living room wagging its tail and knocking over lamps and tables.

H. Monger Burdock

When it comes to the advantages of cats versus dogs as pets, there is no competition. Try going away for a weekend, leaving your German shepherd alone with a bowl of dry food, some water, and a litter box.

Robert Stearns

A dog is prose, a cat is a poem.

Jean Burden

To Someone Very Good and Just,
        Who has proved worthy of her trust,
A Cat will sometimes condescend—
        The Dog is Everybody's Friend.

Oliver Herford

Cats are the ultimate narcissists. You can tell this because of all the time they spend on personal grooming. Dogs aren't like this. A dog's idea of personal grooming is to roll in a dead fish.

James Gorman

The cat, an aristocrat, merits our esteem, while the dog is only a scurvy type who got his position by low flatteries.

Alexandre Dumas

Artists like cats; soldiers like dogs.

Desmond Morris

A cat has a terrific sense of humor, but it sees nothing funny or cute parading in doll's clothes. A dachsund, on the other hand, is delighted to be dressed in little lederhosen and an Alpine sweater.

Robert Stearns

There is the little matter of disposal of droppings in which the cat is far ahead of his rivals. The dog is somehow thrilled by what he or any of his friends have produced, hates to leave it, adores smelling it, and sometimes eats it...The cat covers it up if it can.

Paul Gallico

A cat sleeping on your bed is a far more pleasant companion than a ninety-pound Labrador with bad breath. Furthermore, cats do not snore or break wind.

H. Monger Burdock

The cat lets Man support her. But unlike the dog, she is no hand-licker. Furthermore, unlike Man's other great good friend, the horse, the cat is no sweating serf of Man. The only labor she condescends to perform is to catch mice and rats, and that's fun.

Vance Packard

Among animals, cats are the top-hatted, frock-coated statesmen going about their affairs at their own pace. Dogs are the peasants dutifully plodding behind their leaders.

Robert Stearns

The dog uses smell merely as a medium of information, but the cat revels in it. She will linger near a tree-trunk, smelling each separate aromatic leaf, for the pure pleasure of it, not, like a dog, to trace friend, foe, or prey. If the window of a closed room is opened the cat leans out, smelling the air; new dresses are smelt, partly perhaps for future recognition, but also apparently for pleasure.

Anonymous writer in The Spectator, April 28, 1900

Anybody, but anybody, any lout, any half-wit, any scruffy, self-centered moron, can command the affection and the servile obedience of a dog, but it takes intelligence and understanding—sometimes I think a certain psychic rapport—to win the affection of a cat.

Beverly Nichols

A study of 3,862 children aged between eight and sixteen...found that 18 percent of girls questioned described the cat as the animal they would most like to be, while only 7 percent of boys gave the same response. Dogs, on the contrary, were chosen with almost equal frequency—34 and 32 percent—by both sexes.

James A. Serpell

The tongue of a cat is poison, the tongue of the dog cures.

French proverb

For whereas the dog strives to lessen the distance between himself and man, seeks ever to be intelligent and intelligible, and translates into looks and actions the words he cannot speak, the cat dwells within the circle of her own secret thoughts.

Agnes Repplie

Dogs may fawn on all and some
      As they come;
You, a friend of loftier mind,
Answer friends alone in kind.
Just your foot upon my hand
Softly bids it understand.

Algernon Swinburne

By and large, people who enjoy teaching animals to roll over will find themselves happier with a dog.

Barbara Holland

Again I must remind you that
A Dog's a Dog—A CAT'S A CAT.

T. S. Eliot

The Naming
of Cats

They say the test of literary power is whether a man can write an inscription. I say, "Can he name a kitten?"

Samuel Butler

The naming of cats is an almost infallible guide to the degree of affection bestowed on a cat. Perhaps not affection so much as true appreciation of feline character. You may be reasonably sure when you meet a cat called Ginger or merely Puss that his or her owner has insufficient respect for his cat. Such plebeian and unimaginative names are not given to cats by true cat-lovers.

Michael Joseph

I don't need to apologize for the names we have given our feral cats. I smile when I say, "We named her Turtle because she's a tortoiseshell." It was more complicated than that, and I thought of changing her name when I grew very fond of her. But once it was Turtle it could never be anything else.

All our cats have had additional names. Not the way T. S. Eliot saw it: first the "sensible everyday" name, then the special name peculiar to the particular cat, and finally the name only the cat knows—and ponders raptly for hours on end. No, our cats have always had serveral names, but one name has been a description and not a name: a description we use with ourselves, and not a name we use with the cat. The Honey Puss became His Roundness, and Turtle became Little Miss Meatloaf. I am sorry to say that Herbert, at least to Roy, became the Dim Bulb…And with Sylvester's black hair, long and wild, he became the Dust Mop. Their names were endearments, in their way.

Ellen Perry Berkeley

I named him Caesar, so I could call him Julia's Caesar.

Julia Phillips

One is called Charles, originally Prince Charlie, not after the present holder of that title, but after earlier romantic princes, for he is a dashing and handsome tabby who knows how to present himself.…The other cat, the older brother, with the character of one, has a full ceremonial name, bestowed when he first left kittenhood and his qualities had become evident. We called him General Pinknose the Third, paying tribute, and perhaps reminding ourselves that even the best looked-after cat is going to leave you.

Doris Lessing

.A new kitten has entered our circle, an eight-week-old male blue-point Siamese we have named Sumay. (The meaning of that name is a profoundly secret, extremely deep and personal family affair. It is known to us and the National Security Agency only. I dare not speak of it here.)

Roger Caras

[Freyni] was named after a rock-plant whose identity has long been forgotten by us; but the nurseryman's catalogue said, "Forms a silvery hummock; spreading." The first part of this description fitted her admirably. We couldn't have known in her slim young days how well, in time, the second part would fit.

Monica Edwards

She was called Footy because she always sat on my foot when I was in the kitchen doing some work, and I had to walk about with her on my foot.

Beryl Reid

The most popular feline monikers in the United States:
Males: Smokey, Tiger, Max, Charlie, Rocky, Tigger, Sam/Sammy, Mickey, Toby
Females: Samantha, Misty, Muffin, Fluffy, Patches, Punkin, Missy, Tabitha, Tigger

Survey in *Cat Fancy*

A young man I knew had a cat called "Mother." One day she escaped to the balcony of his fourth-floor apartment and leaped to a ledge on the house next door. He pleaded for her to come home: "Mother, be careful! Don't jump, Mother! Mother, you'll fall!" When Mother's owner looked down at the street below, he found a small crowd staring up at him in horror.

Bruce Morley, D.V.M.

I have three Burmese and I was given my first ever Burmese in 1979 as a first-night present for Pal Joey, the musical...I think it was really smart of me not to call him Joey, because if the play had come off in a week it would have been terrible to be lumbered with a cat named Joey. So he became Spencer, because although Burmese are very amusing, witty, and funny there's something rather grand about them too, so it's a good name for him.

Sian Phillips

The kitten's red hair gave its face a bright Irish look. "Sullavan," pronounced "Su-u-ulllll-a-vann," had a lovely liquid three-syllable value, and would lend itself ideally to crooning and calling, with a long hold, as indicated, on the first syllable. By the time an expert told us that Sullavan was a she, it was too late to change. As a concession we renamed her Miss Sullavan—for the record, that is, not for conversation. For conversation, it was plain Sullavan.

Bryna Ivens Untermeyer

At that point I felt safe in giving him a name, because it looked like the odds in his favor had just risen a good bit. Being newly into yoga, I decided to call him Jai, which means "victory" in Sanskrit. Sanskrit words impart their vibrations to anyone who hears them, and I figured that "Jai" was just what this little squirt needed.

Anitra Frazier

I called my cat William because no shorter name fits the dignity of his character. Poor old man, he has fits now, so I call him Fitz-William.

Josh Billings

The Prophetic Cat

Cats have pawed their way into Budhhist, Muslim, Jewish, and Christian stories.

According to one Buddhist legend, all the animals gathered around Buddha when he died and wept, except for the cat and the snake, who seemed unable to cry. Just when the public wailing hit its peak, a young rat approached one of the oil lamps burning in Buddha's honor and began to lick some of the oil. The temptation proved too much for the cat, who leapt forward and killed the rat. Since killing another animal is a blatant transgression of Buddha's teachings, the cat was punished by not being included among the animals of the Japanese zodiac.

A Muslim story tells of how much Mahomed loved his cat, Meuzza. Called to prayer one day, Mahomed realized that Meuzza was fast asleep on the edge of his robe. Rather than disturb his cat, the holy man cut off the corner of his garment and went on his way.

Cats do not appear anywhere in the official version of the Bible, but they make several appearances in Jewish and Christian apocrypha. One Arabic legend reports that Noah's Ark became overrun with mice and rats because there were no cats aboard. When the situation reached a crisis point, Noah passed his hand three times over the head of a lioness, who sneezed and produced a housecat out of her mouth. Several apocryphal New Testament stories feature a young Jesus in the act of saving cats from angry mobs, and cats and kittens became associated with Jesus and Mary enough to make them a popular addition to medieval and Renaissance nativity paintings.

The Proverbial Cat

Old cats mean young mice.

Italy

Handsome cats and fat dung heaps are the sign of a good farmer.

France

A cat with a straw tail keeps away from fire.

England

A cat with little ones has never a good mouthful.

France

To live long, eat like a cat, drink like a dog.

Germany

When the cat's away, the mice will play.

Western Europe

Curiosity killed the cat,
Satisfaction brought it back!

England

If a girl treads on a cat's tail, she will not find a husband before a year is out.

France

The greedy cat makes the servant girl watchful.

France

In a cat's eyes, all things belong to cats.

England

A scalded cat dreads even cold water.

France

The cat-moon eats the grey mice of night.

Western Europe

A half-penny cat may look at a king.

England

A borrowed cat catches no mice.

Western Europe

Dogs remember faces, cats places.

England

He's as honest as the cat when the meat is out of reach.

England

A cat bitten once by a snake dreads even rope.

Arabia

Wherever the mice laugh at the cat, there you will find a hole.

Portugal

The cat always leaves a mark on his friend.

Spain

All cats are bad in May.

France

The rat stops still when the eyes of the cat shine.

Madagascar

The cat who scratches, scratches for himself.

Russia

The dog wakes three times to watch over his master; the cat wakes three times to strangle him.

France

I gave an order to the cat, and the cat gave it to its tail.

China

Cats are everywhere at home where one feeds them.

Germany

A cat is a lion in a jungle of small bushes.

India

The cat loves fish, but hates wet feet.

Italy

The cat dreams of garbage.

India

A cat has nine lives. For three he plays, for three he strays, and for the last three he stays.

England and America

All cats are gray in the dark.

England

When the cat of the house is black,
The lasses' lovers will have no lack.

England

Sometimes a Cat
Is Just a Cat

Cats represent many different things in historical, religious, and psychological literature. These include fertility, the sun, the moon, evil, vampires, women, female sexuality, the phallus, corn or grain, witches, serpents, demons, and the Virgin Mary.

The Working Cat

While the basic occupation of working cats has always been to hunt and kill rodents, employment conditions and facilities have varied.

As late as 1939, the National Printing Office of France employed a large "staff" of felines to guard the paper supply from the advances of rats and mice. In Vienna, government buildings once had official cats which were retired on small pensions when too old to continue mousing.

The Midway Railway in Trent, England, once employed eight cats to patrol the corn sacks awaiting transportation by rail.

Newspaper cats not only eat mice, but also black beetles that plague paper supplies. The old-style journalistic puss, said to be oblivious to the din of the presses, has been rendered somewhat obsolete by computerized offices.

In the United States, managers of cold-storage warehouses thought that a temperature of six below zero would protect food from vermin, but rats proved to be extremely adaptable, giving birth to long-haired, hungry progeny. Eventually, after losing about four-fifths of the cats they locked into the huge refrigerators, they came up with a hardy race of felines to keep the rats at bay. Agnes Repplier describes them as "little polar bears."

The Mischievous Cat

It's very hard to be polite if you're a cat.

Anonymous

At night he sleeps sprawled at the foot of my bed, where he snores reassuringly until about five in the morning. That's when he gets cuddly: with white paw—claws retracted—he pats my face until I open my eyes. The fact that I then throw him out and slam the door in his face doesn't bother him.

Cathryn Jakobson

Will a cat go to sleep on your face and smother you? Only if you leave the bedroom door open.

Kathleen Fury

Cats find malicious amusement in doing what they know they are not wanted to do, and that with an affectation of innocence that materially aggravates their deliberate offense.

Helen Winslow

I have an Egyptian cat. He leaves a pyramid in every room.

Rodney Dangerfield

The cat surveyed his new home and promptly drove all the rats and mice out of the cave. Once he had finished with them, he started on the food supply. This prompted man to move all his things to a higher watermark, and may have led to the development of the table, which has come to be a bone of contention between cat and man ever since.

Eric Gurney

Whenever we heard a crash in the other room, one of us would say "There's a reason the first three letters of 'catastrophe' are C-A-T!"

St. James Shatzer

He liked to peep into the refrigerator and risked having his head shut in by the closing door. He also climbed to the top of the stove, discontinuing the practice after he singed his tail.

Lloyd Alexander

And such a mess! All the time her cat is prowling the living room and smashing Christmas-tree balls that were not packed away because watching her belt them to smithereens is "the cutest thing." The cutest thing of all, of course, is when she has cuffed one into the bedroom and, in leaping out of bed at night, I come down on it with a bare foot.

Maynard Good Stoddard

Where food was concerned Charles, like all cats, was an incorrigible thief....On one occasion he disgraced us by stealing a cold roast chicken from the house opposite.

Michael Joseph

Cats refuse to take the blame for anything—including their own sins.

Elizabeth Peters

They sleep in the bed and go in and out of the cat door all night—I shudder to think what the laundry thinks we do to our sheets, because it's a sea of mud some nights. If they go in and out a lot all you get are little black pawprints.

Sian Phillips

Most cats, when they are Out want to be In, and vice versa, and often simultaneously.

Louis J. Camuti, D.V.M.

One day he managed to pry the lid off the utility sink and fell into soaking wash. And on another particularly memorable morning, I awoke early and took my first step out of bed, only to land on a five-pound roasting chicken, which I had left in the kitchen sink the previous night to thaw.

Mary Daniels

I am furious with the grey cat. The wicked creature has just robbed me of a young pigeon that I was warming by the fire. The poor little thing was beginning to revive; I had meant to tame it; it would have grown fond of me; and now all this ends in its getting crunched up by a cat. What disappointments there are in life!

Elizabeth Drinker

He went on to tell me about his patent chair. Every time he got up out of it a cat would hop into the seat, and eventually he got fed up with picking cats out of it when he wanted to sit down....So this old boy got four hinges, a bolt, and made a lever that stuck up alongside, clear of one arm. He cut the seat in half, hinging them each side to the frame of the chair. He installed the bolt underneath very securely, wired it strongly to the lever, and that was that.

If a cat got into that chair, all he had to do was to pull the lever, spring the trap, and the cat fell to earth with a bump.

Thurlow Craig

Everyone with experience with cats knows how skillful they are at jumping on to tables and mantelpieces crowded with odds and ends, even though they cannot see them when they begin their jump. Charles had no such skill. Every jump he made was fraught with danger to property and after he had knocked over sundry pieces of valuable glass and china I had to put everything breakable out of his reach. And he was ridiculously proud of his ability to knock things over, to judge by the satisfied expression on his funny little face. Only when a pile of heavy books nearly cascaded on top of him as a result of his efforts to dislodge them did he show any sign of dismay. After two subdued minutes behind the curtain he was at his tricks again.

Michael Joseph

"It's all right, mate," he said. "It's just Smutty's sense of humour. Whenever anyone sleeps in this room he likes to get up on that beam up there, and just as you're dropping off and all's right with the world, leap onto your stomach."

Frank Legg

I had a nefarious old cat, Gyp, who used to open the cupboard door and eat any biscuits accessible. Gyp had a stroke of paralysis, and believed he was going to die. He was in a fright: Mr. Horace Hutchinson observed him and said that this cat justly entertained the most Calvinistic apprehensions of his future reward. Gyp was nursed back into health, as was proved when we found him on the roof of an outhouse with a cold chicken in his possession. Nothing could be more human.

Andrew Lang

Cats rely more on their sense of smell when evaluating immobile objects. Consequently, the sleeping owner (or baby) gets sniffed more often than the awake or moving one. We can see how the normally nocturnal cat, perhaps bored with the lack of activity in the house or aroused by something going on outdoors, seeks out its owners. Finding them fast asleep, it switches to olfactory perception, zeroing in on areas of greatest scent, that is, those with the highest moisture content. Because the mouth and nose provide the most readily available source of scent data, the cat concentrates its efforts on these areas.

Myrna Milani, D.V.M.

We then jointly entered the bathroom, and I encouraged her to use the toilet by firmly holding her on the seat. Nothing. Escaping my clutches, she sought out her own imaginary litter box—right by the front door.

Days passed. Blue was most uncooperative. I fell into despair. I watched her for any sign of concession. In turn, she stopped eating, then ate like there was no Purina. Her bowels went on strike. She began to swell until she resembled the

Astrodome with fur. She stopped playing with her toys, and her legs had stopped supporting her. When she attempted to use the toilet to urinate, she would slide, legs akimbo, not unlike Maury Wills in his heyday, into the bowl.

Lewis Lustman

While we were occupied with new-boat concerns, Misty was busy finding clean places to vomit on. Our bed—a site no doubt chosen to express her opinion of life on the water—received Misty's thorough attention. When she wasn't throwing up, she lay flat, eyes hooded, with a huge beard of mucous that magically reappeared every time we wiped it away.

Herb Payson

Yesterday, a friend called me. When Blue failed to get my attention away from the telephone, she simply "accidentally" walked on the button that hangs the phone up on her way from the bookcase to her water dish. By the time I worked out what she had been up to, she had given herself a bath, dealt with the mice, and instructed my pit bull further on how to keep the male cats in line.

Vicki Hearne

Cats can't help being curious; it's in their genes. I realize that. But if curiosity killed the cat, this one is asking for it. Other cats are curious—this cat is downright nosy. What's inside the sink cupboards? Behind the refrigerator? Down the hot-air registers? On top of the television? Beneath the papers on my desk?

Maynard Good Stoddard

"That's the person who did this," I said, pointing a finger. "She's turning into Ted Bundy. Yesterday she brought in a mouse, the day before that a mole, the day before that a snake, and God only knows how many bodies are buried around here in shallow graves."

"She's a cat," he said.

"Well, that's nice of you to say," I said.

Anne Lamott

Q: What about the way cats claw the upholstery?

A: Learn to like fringe.

Missy Dizick

Some cats will, on occasion, avail themselves of the bathtub for their bodily functions. I have found that two or three inches of cold water in the bottom of the tub tends to discourage cats from this illegal activity.

Milan Greer

Well, Minny is like a teen-aged boy, all right. He's even got a big fantasy life. Only instead of imagining whatever filth teen-aged boys think about, he makes believe he is a lion in the jungle. And I am a fat little antelope. So here I am, hauling a load of dirty clothes to the garage, and this ten-pound lion arches around it like it was a Maypole, and while I am going "Yaah!" and waltzing around with the laundry basket, he disappears underneath the TV.

Modine Gunch

For the armchair authoritarian I recommend some useful remote-control gambits. After a few days of watching them destroy two chairs and one very sturdy floor lamp, I resorted to a pea-shooter. It took some practice at first, but eventually I could pick off a recalcitrant kitten at twenty paces from the coffee table.

Milan Greer

One day when I was paying an urgent visit to the loo...I was absolutely rushing, but he beat me to it by about two seconds, and shot under me as I was about to sit down, and, of course, almost got a concussion, because he went crashing to the bottom of the basin of the loo and raised a big lump on his head. He was extremely heavy to lift out, because he'd swallowed a great deal of water.

Beryl Reid

I could half persuade myself that the word felonius is derived from the feline temper.

Robert Southey

At about four o'clock in the morning, I was awakened. Something was treading—leisurely, thoughtfully, and determinedly—on a part of me never before trod upon. A street lamp shone into the room and was reflected by two great blue disembodied coals burning at me. It was the cat; his claws were unsheathed, and I arose with strangled cries of pain. I know that the castrato once had his place in opera, but that was centuries ago.

Gilbert Millstein

The other cats had always been skillful in picking their way along crowded shelves or tables. Moira found it more agreeable to push objects out of her path. Her enjoyment at hanging onto lamp cords was only dampened by the crash of the light bulbs.

Lloyd Alexander

To the pussy we're indebted
For upholstered chairs all shredded,
For that all-pervading stink
For the box beneath the sink…

William Rossa Cole

Sometimes, protesting a four-hour absence, Sweetheart has rolled up the living room rug and stuffed it in the corner. On other occasions, he has played a fabulous game with an entire roll of toilet paper.

Cathryn Jakobson

Cats have intercepted my footsteps at the ankle for so long that my gait, both at home and on tour, has been compared to that of a man wading through low surf.

Roy Blount, Jr.

Many cats react with inappropriate defecation and urination when something suddenly changes in their life. This may be the addition of a new cat, the arrival of a new family member (e.g., a baby), or a change in daily routine. Depending on the severity of the change and on the cat's general ability to adapt, inappropriate defecation and urination can disappear quickly or remain a problem.

Claudia Mertens and Rosemarie Schar

Cats can be very funny, and have the oddest ways of showing they're glad to see you. Rudimace always peed in our shoes.

W. H. Auden

Play with live and dead prey is common in the domestic cat, but also occurs in wild adult felids. Cat owners, who do not tolerate play with live prey, can take the prey item away from the cat and replace it with a substitute play object; of course, they will then have to dispose of the prey animal themselves.

Claudia Mertens and Rosemarie Schar

A cat playing is normal behavior; a cat playing on your head at four o'clock in the morning is not appropriate behavior from a human point of view.

Dale Olm, D.V.M.

That cat! I wish she were dead! But I can't shorten her days, because, you see, my poor, dear wee dog liked her. Well, there she is! And as long as she attends Mr. C. at his meals (and she doesn't care a sheaf of tobacco for him at any other time), so long will Mr. C. continue to give her bits of meat and driblets of milk, to the ruination of carpets and hearthrugs! I have over and over again pointed out to him the stains she has made, but he won't believe them her doings....So what I wish is that you would shut up the poor creature when Mr. C. has breakfast, dinner or tea; and if he remarks on her absence, say it was my express wish.

Jane Carlyle, wife of English writer
Thomas Carlyle, in a letter to her housekeeper

What about nocturnal fighting and howling? Because most of this commotion attends mating, trying to eliminate this behaviorally proves most unrewarding. However these displays do respond to surgical treatment.

Myrna Milani, D.V.M.

Why, then if not to steal food, would a cat go up on the counter? Why did George Mallory try to go up on Mount Everest, which was quite a lot more trouble? Because it is there. Because of the view from the kitchen window. To lick the drips from the tap in the sink. To try to pry open the cupboards and see what's inside them, maybe to squeeze among the glassware. Or, on a rainy day, to look for small objects to knock off onto the floor and see if they roll.

Barbara Holland

Cat Suits

Over the years, cases concerning cats have generated considerable fees for the legal profession.

In 1973, Dr. William Grier of San Diego bequeathed $415,000 to his two fifteen-year-old cats, Hellcat and Brownie. In 1975, Ivy Blackhurst of Sheffield, England, also honored her cat Blackie with a bequest of £22,000.

Some litigation springs from natural feline preying instincts. In 1924, an Oklahoman named Helsel shot a white persian cat who was killing his prized Plymouth Rock chickens. The cat's owner, a man named Fletcher, successfully sued Helsel for $150 to compensate for the cat's death. An 1887 case in Scotland featured a plaintiff named Webb asking £1 in damages for his carrier pigeon, killed by a Mr. McFeat's cat. Webb lost his case because he had not watched over his bird carefully, but the judge did not require him to pay court costs because Mr. McFeat had initially denied that his cat had performed the dirty deed.

When food stores still employed cats to control rodent populations, ailurophobic customers had a tendency to sue. In 1921, a Mrs. Goodwin failed to convince a court that the store cat at the E. B. Nelson Grocery in Massachussetts had bitten her. Store employees failed to agree that the cat was vicious, and during the hearing Mrs. Goodwin was forced to admit that she had brought her dog with her, who had attacked the cat. Another failed suit was that of Ruth Pallman in 1933, who charged that a Connecticut A&P store's cat had attacked her.

The strangest case of feline litigation surrounds Arthur, a British television star of cat food commercials (a sort of U.K. version of Morris the Cat), whose owner refused to lend him to the cat food company to make more commercials. He alleged that the company had removed his cat's teeth in order to force him to dip his paws into the cat food cans on camera. Eventually a court ruled that the cat food company actually owned Arthur, but in 1968 the owner deposited the famous feline in the Russian Embassy to keep him out of the jurisdiction of the British courts.

The Best Cat in the World

Mad Anthony was the only cat I knew who sprang straight up. He never leaped toward a butterfly, bug, or bird. He rose vertically, at least two feet, often three. Whether there was wildlife nearby or not. There was no warning, and the effect was startling. When Mad Anthony sprang, it was as if he'd been standing on a land mine. All of a sudden—boingg!

Derek Williamson

I have just been called to the door by the sweet voice of Toss, whose morning proceedings are wonderful. She sleeps—She has just jumped on my lap, and her beautiful tail has made this smudge, but I have put her down again. I was going to say that she sleeps on an arm-chair before the drawing-room fire; descends the moment she hears the servants about in the morning, and makes them let her out; comes back and enters Flu's room with Eliza regularly at half-past seven. Then she comes to my door and gives a mew, and then—especially if I let her in, and go on writing or reading without taking any notice of her—there is a real demonstration of affection, such as never again occurs in the day. She purrs, she walks round and round me, she jumps in my lap, she turns to me and rubs her head and nose against my chin, she opens her mouth and raps her pretty white teeth against my pen. Then she leaps down, settles herself by the fire, and never shows any more affection all day.

Matthew Arnold

Sam raised his paw for all the world as if he were about to protest, and then, apparently thinking better of it, he pretended instead that the action had been only for the purpose of commencing his nightly wash.

Walter de la Mare

A morning kiss, a discreet touch of his nose landing somewhere on the middle of my face. Because his long white whiskers tickled, I began every day laughing.

Janet F. Faure

He always came when I called, meowing happily in a voice that was a cross between a cat's and a child's. More like a dog than a cat in his loyalty and lack of traditional aloofness, Miki also seemed more human than a dog. If Miki thought of himself as a person, I encouraged him. He understood my moods and forgave them, curling up beside me after my childhood temper tantrums, trusting me to be gentle with him even though I had been yelling moments before.

Andrea Higbie

I always know when Brutus is getting all geared up for one of his "crazies." His usually china-blue eyes somehow turn into blazing, reddened orbs, and he takes off like a grey-hound out of the starting box, fairly flying up and down the stairs. It honestly seems as though his paws are barely touching the ground as he tears through the house.

Lynn Allison

Eponine, with her sea-green eyes, her narrow face, her impertinent nose, her small and delicate limbs, had an air of distinction which charmed Gautier's appreciative friends. She was a polite little cat, rather fond of company, and would receive his guests with cordial pleasure, purring as she stepped from one chair to another, as though to say: "Don't be impatient. Look at the pictures, or talk to me, if I amuse you. My master is coming down." On his appearance, she would retire discreetly to an armchair, or to a corner of the piano, and listen to the conversation without interrupting it, being French, and accustomed to good society.

If Gautier dined alone, Eponine's place was laid opposite to his; and, when he came into the dining-room, he found her always in her chair, waiting serenely for his arrival. She would place her forepaws daintily on the edge of the table, and present her smooth forehead to be kissed, "like a well-bred little girl who is affable and affectionate to relatives and old people."

Agnes Repplier

Max—this is embarassing to write about in public—licks my feet. I never lick them myself, but I catch a whiff of them now and then, and that proves to me that Max must adore me.

Kathleen Fury

Monster was the most self-consciously dignified cat I ever knew. If, during a sociable conversation with someone he liked, in which Monster was usually a happy participant, I laughed suddenly, all the delight was instantly wiped from Monnie's expressive eyes. It was absolutely necessary to tell him, "I'm laughing with you, Monnie, not at you."

Winifred Carriere

In all my earlier years I used frequently to see my father come home in the dusk, rather fagged with his round of teaching; and, after dining, he would lie down flat on the hearth-rug, close by the fire, snoring vigorously. Beside him would stand up our old familiar tabby cat, poised on her haunches, and holding on by her fore-claws inserted into the fender-wires, warming her furry front. Her attitude (I have never seen any feline imitation of it) was peculiar—somewhat in the shape of a capital Y. "The cat making the Y" was my father's phrase for this performance. She was the mother of a numerous progeny. One of her daughters—also long an inmate of our house—was a black and white cat named Zoe by my elder sister Maria, who had a fancy for anything Greekish; but Zoe never made a Y.

William Rossetti

The difficulty of catering to her is so well understood by tradesmen that recently, when the housemaid carried her on an errand to the grocery—Agrippina is very fond of these jaunts and of the admiration she excites—the grocer, a fatherly man, with cats of his own, said briskly, "Is this the little lady who eats the biscuits?" and presented her on the spot with several choice varieties from which to choose. She is fastidious, too, about the way in which her meals are served; disliking any other dishes than her own, which are of blue-and-white china; requiring that her meat be cut up fine and all the fat removed, and that her morning oatmeal should be well sugared and creamed. Milk she holds in scorn. My friends tell me sometimes that it is not the common custom of cats to receive so much attention at table, and that it is my fault Agrippina is so exacting; but such grumblers fail to take into consideration the marked individuality that is the charm of every kindly treated puss.

Agnes Repplier

She soon turned into a rather portly cat whose pale yellow eyes became hot pools of luminescent greens when she met my headlights late at night. Almost from the beginning she displayed an even temper. She made her way through dogs and children with unruffled dignity. She washed both sides of her face with her left paw, and when I scratched the spot at the base of her spine that she couldn't reach herself, she lifted her face in ecstasy and stuck out her tongue.

Irving Townsend

Polar Bear did not like change. He was, when you came right down to it, a very Republican cat—he did not like anything to happen which had not happened before.

Cleveland Amory

The Quotable Cat

I recollect him one day scrambling up Dr. Johnson's breast, apparently with much satisfaction, while my friend, smiling and half-whistling, rubbed down his back, and pulled him by the tail; and when I observed he was a fine cat, saying, "Why, yes, Sir, but I have had cats whom I liked better than this"; and then, as if perceiving Hodge to be out of countenance, adding, "but he is a very fine cat, a very fine cat indeed."

James Boswell

Webster was very large and very black and very composed. He conveyed the impression of being a cat of deep reserves. Descendent of a long line of ecclesiastical ancestors who had conducted their decorous courtships beneath the shadow of cathedrals and on the back walls of bishops' palaces, he had that exquisite poise which one sees in the high dignitaries of the Church.

P. G. Wodehouse

Sonny was so fat that people gasped as she entered the room. Once my mother gave her one of those fake pearl collars, which made her look like an obese matron on her way to the opera.

C. E. Crimmins

Nora, my cat, is old, maybe fourteen or fifteen, but her wrinkles don't show.

Sylvia Plachy

Silver Paws had a way with the ladies…a frolicsome kitten whose sense of humor was unbalanced by a proper sense of dignity, he artfully won all hearts and easily became the center of attraction wherever he appeared.

N. Margaret Campbell

Squid, for all her play acting, is a lover. She often does such intense figure eights around our ankles it becomes all but impossible to walk and that's not just when she wants food, either. She appears from nowhere when you are trying to read or watch television and jumps into your lap or climbs up onto your shoulders to drape herself to sleep there. You wake up and find out that she has been sharing your pillow.

Roger Caras

Caesar and I kind of hit adolescence together. While he howls and rests his burning balls on the shady part of the hood of my father's car, I torment my parents with a stream of big-chested pea-brained wonders. It is not an era of neutering, so Caesar walks on the wild side. While I engage in hours of tongue kissing and heavy petting he goes out and gets laid.

Julia Phillips

Above his nose, Mr. Forsyte has a bald patch which is often dusted with earth and sand when he comes in. Both patch and dusting are due to snuffling down rabbit-holes, a terrifying experience, surely for the inmates; worse, I should think, than a wolf at one's door, since rabbits have no doors.

Monica Edwards

The Persecuted Cat

Should ever anything be missed—milk, coals, umbrellas, brandy—The cat's pitched into with a boot or anything that's handy.

C. S. Calverley

For centuries, proverbial wisdom has identified cats with women and the more threatening aspects of female sexuality. The unmitigated cruelty cats have received as a result of this metaphor doubtless speaks volumes about the sexual insecurities of European males.

James A. Serpell

The car has changed the cat's life as much as it has our own, killed far more than the Inquisition, and made prisoners of cared-for cats in populous areas.

Barbara Holland

CAT: n. A soft, indestructible automation provided by nature to be kicked when things go wrong in the domestic circle.

Ambrose Bierce

In spite of the veneration which the Egyptians had for the cat, we are told that the punishment for adultery by a woman in Egypt was to be sewn into a sack with a live cat and flung into the Nile.

Mildred Kirk

I once had an aunt who kept saying that there was more than one way to skin a cat. One day, during a heat wave on the East Side of New York, she yielded to this impulse, and a few hours later a gent wearing a white coat came and carted her away. She was still holding the cat's skin. It wasn't a pretty sight.

Groucho Marx

A Spanish courtier, Juan Cristoval, wrote about a "cat organ" played by a bear that appeared at a street pageant in Brussels in 1549: "In place of pipes, it had twenty cats separately confined in narrow cases, from which they could not stir. Their tails were tied to cords attached to the keyboard of the organ. When the bear pounded the keys, the cords were jerked, and this pulled the tails of the cats, and made them mew in bass or treble notes, according to the nature of the airs."

Cats are oppressed; dogs terrify them, landladies starve them, boys stone them, everybody speaks of them with contempt. If they were human beings we could talk of their oppressors with a studied violence, add our strength to theirs, even organize the oppressed and like good politicians sell our charity for power.

W. B. Yeats

This area is known as cat country to the cat dealers and stealers. I suppose they drive around it and take any animals they like the look of which are not safely indoors. It happens at night; and it is unpleasant to think how the thieves keep the cats quiet so that they don't wake their owners. The people of this street suspect the hospitals by which we are surrounded. Those vivisectionists have been again, they say; and perhaps they are right.

Doris Lessing

According to superstition, the tail was the source of the cat's supernatural powers, and it was common practice in Japan to cut off kittens' tails to prevent them turning into demons later in life.

James Serpell

Put the cat in the pot, hold the lid down with the left hand, let it boil for twenty-four hours and then, having placed the meat in a new dish, throw it over your shoulder and watch yourself 'til you no longer see yourself in a mirror.

Recipe for making a person invisible, *The Devil's Bible*, France

Although embalmed cats are now sold for dissection, until recently in some universities, students were simply given a bottle of chloroform and told to go out and get their own cat.

Kathleen Kilgore

The cat, loving though it could be, had retained a wildness and independence of its own, and when the witch-cult fever struck Europe it became easy for people to identify it with the witches. It has been the cat's tragedy.

Katharine Briggs

I've thrown a lot of things at the cats who stray into my yard, but ice cubes work best—they're readily available near the kitchen back door, hard enough to hurt, and leave no evidence.

Thomas Maeder

Depriving cats of REM sleep didn't prove easy for researchers, who had to wake the subjects up every time a polygraph showed the start of REM sleep patterns....The cats were able to sleep even on treadmills. The only method that finally worked involved placing cats on a bucket surrounded by cold water, so that when the body lost muscle tone in REM sleep, the animal fell in.

Kathleen Kilgore

Bad Calendar Dates for Cats

Shrove Tuesday

Every Shrove Tuesday-eve at Store Magleby near Copenhagen, a live cat was imprisoned in a barrel at which horsemen tilted...In the English village of Albrighton a cat was annually whipped to death on Shrove Tuesday.

Margaret Kirk

St. John's Day

It was also in Metz, in 1344...thirteen cats were burned alive in an iron cage as a remedy for an epidemic of St. Vitus' dance....The next morning the epidemic had miraculously ceased. It was then that the magistrates decided that the best way to hunt Satan out of his feline shape was to burn the cat alive. They proceeded to organize a ritual burning. For a long time afterwards, on every eve of Saint John, the people of Metz commemorated this victory by lighting a great bonfire and throwing onto it the fateful number of thirteen living cats....In Paris, from 1471, Louis XI used to attend the fires of Saint John with great flourish and ceremony for the simple pleasure of watching two dozen cats burned alive.

Fernand Mery

The Entire Month of May

At Ypres during the Middle Ages two or three cats were thrown from the cathedral belfry every second Sunday in May.

Mildred Kirk

May cats catch no mice, and one is well-advised to drown May kittens at birth, for they will take toads and spiders into the house, and those that do so are not natural cats but witches in disguise.

Interview with villager in *Somerset Folklore*, by Ruth Tongue

Agrarian Perils

The peasants of Russia, Poland, and Bohemia buried a cat alive in the cornfields to guarantee a good crop.

In Transylvania and Bohemia, farmers killed black tom-cats and buried them in the fields on Christmas Eve and at the sowing of the first seed in spring to prevent evil spirits from harming the crops.

Throughout Europe, it was customary to bury black cats under fruit trees to stimulate growth.

Superstitions

WEATHER

A drowned cat is the surest way to raise a favorable wind.

England

If a cat washes behind its ears, it will rain.

England

If a cat leaves a sunny corner and goes to sleep in the barn, it will rain.

England

When a cat's whiskers droop, rain is coming.

England

LUCK

To see a white cat on the road is lucky.

America

Seeing a white cat on the way to school will bring trouble that day.

England

It is bad luck to see a white cat at night.

America

A cat on the doorstep brings bad luck.

Norway

A strange black cat on your porch brings prosperity.

Scotland

If a black cat chooses to make its home with you, you will have good luck.

England and America

It is bad luck to cross a stream carrying a cat.

France

Dreaming of a white cat means good luck.

America

Never stroke a cat backward, or your luck will turn bad.

America

It is bad luck to put the cat out before you wind the clock.

Wales

To kill a cat brings seventeen years of bad luck.

Ireland

To step over a cat brings bad luck.

America

PROPHECY

A tortoiseshell cat climbing a tree foretells death by accident.

France

If a black cat lies on the bed of a sick man, he will surely die.

Italy

Those who dislike cats will be carried to the cemetery in the rain.

Ireland and Holland

If a cat appears on a grave of a buried person, his or her soul is in the Devil's power.

Western Europe

To dream of a black cat at Christmastime foretells a serious illness during the coming year.

Germany

A black cat crossing one's path by moonlight means death in an epidemic.

Ireland

A cat sneezing is a good omen for everyone who hears it.

Italy

Those who mistreat cats will have umbrellas at their weddings.

Ireland and Holland

SYMBOLISM

In dreams, cats mean craftiness.

America

REMEDIES AND INSTRUCTIONS

To keep a cat at home, put a piece of food under your armpit and give it to him to eat.

Amish belief, America

To keep a cat from straying, put butter on its feet.

British Isles and America

When moving to a new home, always put the cat through the window instead of the door, so that it will not leave.

America

If scared by a cat, collect hair from a cat or a dog and burn it under your nose.

Lithuania

When you see a one-eyed cat, spit on your thumb, stamp it in the palm of your hand, and make a wish. The wish will come true.

America

To keep a stray cat at your house, put some hair from her tail under the doorsill.

Yugoslavia

The
Playful Cat

No one can have experienced to the fullest the true sense of achievement and satisfaction who has never pursued and successfully caught his tail.

Rosalind Welcher

Although all cat games have their rules and ritual, these vary with the individual player. The cat, of course, never breaks a rule. If it does not follow precedent, that simply means it has created a new rule and it is up to you to learn it quickly if you want the game to continue.

Sidney Denham

We entertain each other with mutual follies, and if I have my time to begin or to refuse, she also has hers.

Montaigne

Of all the toys available, none is better designed than the owner himself. A large multipurpose plaything, its parts can be made to move in almost any direction. It comes completely assembled and it makes a sound when you jump on it.

Stephen Baker

Cats do not need to be shown how to have a good time, for they are unfailingly ingenious in that respect.

James Mason

It is axiomatic that you cannot order a cat to play. You can only coax and beguile.

Sidney Denham

I usually initiate one of our regular biting fights. In these, during the cold weather I cover him with a blanket and in warm weather with a sheet. And then, while I come at him with my fingers from different directions from above, he bites from below. If I get him down with one hand before he draws blood, I win. If he gets a good finger bite lockhold, however—albeit a bloodless one—it's a draw.

Cleveland Amory

There is nothing in the animal world, to my mind, more delightful than grown cats at play. They are so swift and light and graceful, so subtle and designing, and yet so richly comic.

Monica Edwards

But the kitten, how she starts,
Crouches, stretches, paws and darts!

William Wordsworth

To see Boy play ball with a piece of cork is a truly wonderful study in curves and intensest vitality. He crouches just about three yards from his master, the pupils of his eyes expanded till they look like black wells, with the merest rim of green, his tail beating the deck with a regular circular movement.

"Ready, Boy!" cries the Captain, and he stiffens himself with a joyous quiver which runs through the whole of the lithe body, in which every atom of life is gathered for the spring; it is for the time a matter of life and death, and his whole being is aflame with ardour; there he is himself, and the cork, and incidentally, the man who throws—nothing else, and no one else in the whole of the wide world.

"Now!" The cork is flung and Boy springs, stretched to his full length, then gathered to a ball in mid-air with front paws upraised like a cricketer's hands, full a yard from the deck, catches the cork between his white-stockinged feet, and rolls on the deck, kicking at it in a perfect transport of delight with his hind-feet.

But if he misses? Ah, that is another matter. Supposing we are too well-mannered to laugh, he simply appears oblivious of the bauble having been thrown at all, but walks the deck a little, goes up to it in a leisurely fashion, sniffs as if to say, "What in the world can this be?" looks at his master— "a game, eh?" and finally picking it up, deposits it at his feet, asking, as an obviously new idea, that it shall be thrown. But if anyone, other than his master, has laughed, the game is over for the day, and off goes his Highness in a fit of sulks.

Elinor Mordan

A feather lightly brandished close to his nose will tempt even the veteran in retirement.

Michael Joseph

Cats are notoriously sore losers. Coming in second best, especially to someone as poorly coordinated as a human being, grates their sensibility.

Stephen Baker

Cat Naps

Cats sleep an average of 14.8 hours per day.
Humans sleep an average of 7.5.

Cats are rather delicate creatures and they are subject to a
good many ailments, but I never heard of one who suffered
from insomnia.

Joseph Wood Krutch

The cat sees through shut lids.

English Proverb

A little drowsing cat is an image of perfect beatitude.

Champfleury

There are people who reshape the world by force or argument, but the cat just lies there, dozing, and the world quietly reshapes itself to suit his comfort and convenience.

Allen and Ivy Dodd

She is a Presence, in bed. She snores: soft little wheezings. She talks in her sleep: closed-mouth little mutterings full of expression and complaint and observation. And she is an opportunist, setting her weight against the nearest body and pushing ever closer as the chance arises.

Ellen Perry Berkeley

Most beds sleep up to six cats. Ten cats without the owner.

Stephen Baker

Sleeping together is a euphemism for people but tantamount to marriage with cats.

Marge Piercy

I wish you could see the two cats drowsing side by side in a Victorian nursing chair, their paws, their ears, their tails complementally adjusted, their blue eyes blinking open on a single thought of when I shall remember it's their suppertime. They might have been composed by Bach for two flutes.

Sylvia Townsend Warner

A sleeping cat is ever alert.

Fred Schwab

Drowsing, they take the noble attitude of a great sphinx who...sleeps always, dreaming dreams that have no end.

Charles Pierre Baudelaire

In my experience, cats and beds seem to be a natural combination.

Louis J. Camuti, D.V.M.

Some ten to thirty minutes after initially falling asleep, the cat will usually go into the second sleep state which is sometimes referred to as deep sleep or active sleep. All muscles of the body, including those of the neck, become completely atonic. Therefore the body becomes slack. During this sleep state there are bursts of rapid eye movements in either the vertical or horizontal direction. Along with the eye movements there may be rapid flexing of the paws, occasional scratching motions, rapid movement of the ears or whiskers or tail, or movements of the legs.

Benjamin L. Hart, D.V.M.

A cat pours his body on the floor like water. It is restful just to see him.

William Lyon Phelps

You can't look at a sleeping cat and feel tense.

Jane Pauley

He seems the incarnation of everything soft and silky and velvety, without a sharp edge in his composition, a dreamer whose philosophy is sleep and let sleep.

Saki

A cat sleeps fat, yet walks thin.

Fred Schwab

For in the stillness a cat languishes loudly.

William Ernest Henley

Cats everywhere asleep on the shelves like motorized book ends.

Audrey Thomas

The cat pretends to sleep the better to see.

Chateaubriand

You all day long, beside the fire,
Retrace in dreams your dark desire.

Arthur Benson

A Room with a Mew

Guests at the Anderson Hotel in Wabasha, Minnesota, can request feline "loaners" when they check in. The hotel has fifteen cats available as sleeping companions for hotel residents. Owner John Hall says that one in five guests wants to share a bed with a feline.

"They are as common as a bucket of ice would be in other hotels," says Hall, who does not charge for the service. He says that the cats are all taken, every weekend.

In Their Own Words

Personally, I don't believe felines are a fad. We're here to stay.

Morris, spokescat for Purina Nine Lives cat food

They say a cat always lands on his feet, but they don't mention the pain.

Garfield, cartoon personality

Well, then, a dog growls when it's angry and wags its tail when it's pleased. Now, I growl when I'm pleased and wag my tail when I'm angry. Therefore I'm mad.

Cheshire Cat in *Alice's Adventures in Wonderland* by Lewis Carroll

Sufferin' succotash!

Whether or not you wish to take over the bed is entirely up to you, and here again you will find yourself involved in that astonishing ambivalence that seems to be a part of people and that never ceases to surprise me, even while I welcome it. They won't want you on the bed, and at the same time, they will want you on the bed. If this is a paradox it is because that is what people seem to be like.

x.x.x.x.x.x.x., feline "author" of Paul Gallico's *The Silent Miaow*

The life of a female
artist is continually
hampered what in hell
have I done to deserve
all these kittens

Mehitabel, alley cat friend of Archy, author/cockroach of Don
Marquis' imagination

I am the Cat which fought near the Persea Tree in Annu on the night when the foes of Neb-er-tcher were destroyed.

Feline representative of Egyptian god Ra, quoted in a papyrus from
1580 B.C.

As a housepet, I'm overqualified!

> Cat in Stephen Baker's *How to Live with a Neurotic Cat*

Nothing can beat this recipe (Beetle Butter Crunch) for a snack or a quick bite. I have found that it tastes best when prepared with beetles. However, when they are not in season, roaches or water bugs will do.

> Chef Whiskers, *Favorite Cat Recipes* by Carl Logan

Are we men, or arrre we mice?

> Sylvester, in *Kitty Kornered*, 1946

A big yellow tomcat with a torn ear and his face criss-crossed with love and battle scars—believe me, I know THAT type—came up to me and said, "Hello Goddess! How are things?" I spit in his eye. I don't allow anyone to take liberties with me.

> Thomasina, in Paul Gallico's *Thomasina*

People make great companions for cats because they practically take care of themselves...all a cat has to do is purr and rub against their legs every now and then and they're content. I get such a kick out of watching humans play, too—when they're running around in the morning late for work, when they're ripping through stacks of bills.

> Morris

I had to devise another manner of writing, suited to the construction of my small right paw. And find a new method I did, as may well be imagined. This is how great inventions and discoveries are born.

Another grave difficulty for me was how to dip the pen into the inkpot. For I was unable to keep my paw clean during this operation since it always got into the ink as well. The first strokes, made with my paw rather than with the pen, always appeared smudged and sprawling. This might lead foolish people to see in my first manuscripts little more than paper spattered with ink. But, the intelligent man will readily detect in those early works a cat of great depth, and will be astonished, even delighted, by the profundity and the richness of intellect which came gushing from its inexhaustible spring.

> Cat Murr, the cat who learned to read and write
> in E. T. A. Hoffman's *The Opinions of Tom Cat Murr*

One little bird...just one! Just one! I—I—I can't stand it...I gotta have a bird...I'm weak...I'm weak...But I don't care! I can't help it! After all, I am a pussycat.

> Sylvester, in *Birds Anonymous*, 1957

Show me a good mouser, and I'll show you a cat with bad breath.

Garfield

Whatever you do, don't treat us like dogs. We don't fetch slippers or newspapers. If you want a servant, hire a hound. If your cat rolls over and plays dead, you're in trouble. We don't need authority figures like canines do.

Morris

We are the Unscratchables.

Top Cat

I will be kind to the Baby while I am in the Cave, as long as he does not pull my tail too hard, for always and always, and always. But still I am the Cat that walks by himself, and all places are alike to me.

The Cat in "The Cat that Walked by Himself,"
Just So Stories, Rudyard Kipling

Pussy said to the Owl, "You elegant fowl!
How charmingly sweet you sing!
O let us be married! too long we have tarried:
But what shall we do for a ring?"

From Edward Lear's *Owl and the Pussy-Cat*

One helpful hint I would like to share with you about all bird recipes is this: Never try to substitute with a bluejay. They are quite nasty and will fight back.

Chef Whiskers, *Favorite Cat Recipes*

I am the Cat of Cats. I am
The everlasting cat!

William Brighty Rands

The Purr

To err is human,
To purr feline.

Robert Byrne

Old Force has a purr with an enormous range of volume, from shouting-loud to so soft that it is virtually inaudible. This latter is known as Force Purring in Overdrive, and is an expression of the utmost in contentment. At such times the person on whose lap he is resting can feel the vibration of the dynamo, can even see the faintest tremor of the flanks, but can hear no sound at all.

Monica Edwards

A typical cat quirk is that they can purr. We don't pretend to know what kind of mechanism goes into the making of a purr, or how to wind it up once it runs down. However, this much is known: There are a wide variety of purrs which range from the almost inaudible to the kind which can be felt through the floor. Loud purring might possibly set up sympathetic vibrations in a building and send it crashing to the ground. For these reasons, as well as others too numerous to mention, lions make very poor household pets.

Eric Gurney

To please himself only the cat purrs.

Irish proverb

"Four" has the best purr I have ever known, bar none, a purr with a quite astonishing vocal range. If he were not called "Four" I should call him "Callas," because his purr really has a prima donna quality.

Beverley Nichols

It is a very inconvenient habit of kittens (Alice had once made the remark) that, whatever you say to them, they always purr.

Lewis Carroll

They purr to signal a relaxed, friendly mood. And their purring may also help relax them and those around them who feel and hear their purring—like getting a nice massage in sound.

Michael W. Fox, D.V.M.

A cat can be trusted to purr when she is pleased, which is more than can be said for human beings.

William Ralph (Dean) Inge

It was difficult to feel vexed by a creature that burst into a chorus of purring as soon as I spoke to him.

Philip Brown

Purring would seem to be, in her case, an automatic safety-valve device for dealing with happiness overflow.

Monica Edwards

The perfect cat is one with a purr that doesn't wake you up in the middle of the night.

Alan Forman

How Cats Came to Purr

by Anne Kaier

God was making cats. God made orange cats. God made black cats. God made calico cats.

He gave cats paws. He gave cats ears. He gave cats tails. He did not give cats purrs, yet.

God made faces for the cats. God painted faces on the orange cats. He painted faces on the black cats. He painted faces on the calico cats.

The cats were beautiful.

God smiled. He sat back on his stool. He folded his arms.

He thought for a while.

Then he said, "Cats need brains, too."

God kept the brains in a clay pot. He scooped out some brains. He gave some brains to each orange cat. He gave some brains to each black cat. He was giving some brains to each calico cat.

Lucille was the smallest calico cat. She was at the end of the line.

God looked at Lucille. He looked into his pot. There were only a few brains left.

God said, "There are only a few brains left. There are not enough for Lucille."

Lucille said, "That's OK, God. I am very pretty. I don't need brains."

God said, "I know you are pretty. But you need something else."

God kept the purrs in a blue box. He took out a purr very gently. He slid the purr into Lucille's neck. Lucille purred aloud.

Then all the other cats wanted purrs, too.

God gave all the cats purrs. God smiled. And all the cats purred.

Goodbyes

Because a man is higher up on the evolutionary scale than the cat doesn't necessarily mean that a man's death is more painful for those he leaves than for those who have lost a cat. Should one mourn more for an indifferent uncle than for a devoted and loving pet? It would be a strange person who did so.

Louis J. Camuti, D.V.M.

Insofar as a cat can think, Lily was, I believe, bewildered. She didn't understand what had happened to her lithe and supple body, her appetite, her control. She only "knew" in that profound way animals do seem to know, that something was terribly wrong—and she turned to us for help.

MaryHelene P. Rosenbaum

I will always remember the olive-eyed tabby who taught me that not all relationships are meant to last a lifetime. Sometimes just an hour is enough to touch your heart.

Barbara L. Diamond

No amount of time can erase the memory of a good cat, and no amount of masking tape can ever totally remove his fur from your couch.

Leo Dworken

Sometimes I think about what Midgie is doing in her next life. If Shirley MacLaine is right, I might get a chance to clean her litter box all over again.

Winifred Stockman

Life is cruel. My favorite cats have always been the stupid ones, and they end up getting run over way before their time.

Alan Forman

Dynasties of cats, as numerous as the dynasties of the Pharaohs, succeeded each other under my roof. One after another they were swept away by accident, by flight, by death. All were loved and regretted; but oblivion is our common fate, and the memory of the cats we have lost fades like the memory of men.

Theophile Gautier

No heaven will not ever Heaven be
Unless my cats are there to welcome me.

Epitaph in a pet cemetery

The only thing that eases the pain is remembering how he jumped up on the counter and gulped down a half pound of expensive goat's cheese just three hours before he died. I should have counted on him to go in style.

C. E. Crimmins

The habits are still hard to break. I come into the house looking for Miki's welcome. I'll be half-asleep and see a clump of blanket on the bed and reach to pet it. Noises in the night make me think he's walking through the room, checking to be sure that everything is as it should be and that I am safe. Or I'll be sitting on the couch and think I've felt him lightly spring up beside me, and a warm rush fills me until I remember he's dead.

Andrea Higbie

Unlike many humans in the same position, he never wrote his memoirs of his days in the White House and never discussed them for quotation, though he was privy to many official secrets.

Obituary in *Alexandria Gazette* for Tom Kitten,
President John F. Kennedy's cat

Bernice went into a coma and I went out to the backyard to dig a hole. When I got back she was on her feet again, and the whole summer before her death she amused herself by literally jumping in and out of the grave.

Bruce Schimmel

A mouse.
Some yarn.
A moth.
A fly.
But now he's gone:
Kitty,
Goodbye.

Ann Carson

Joey's gone from here,
But somewhere now a kitten's born
With Joey's joyous spirit. Sing!
Do not mourn.

Winifred Carriere

I often stop when I'm driving to pause a minute and look at Tom's grave and remember him....He was a great cat and a good soldier.

Louis J. Camuti, D.V.M.

We did all in our power to save him. The doctor felt his pulse, sounded his lungs, and ordered him ass's milk. He drank it with ready obedience out of his own special saucer. For hours he lay upon my knee like the shadow of a sphinx. I felt his spine under my finger tips like the beads of a rosary, and he tried to respond to my caresses with a feeble and rattling purr. On the day of his death he was lying panting upon his side, when suddenly, and as though by a supreme effort, he arose and staggered weakly towards me. His great eyes were wide-stretched, and raised to mine with a look of agonized supplication, as though they said: "Save me, save me, you who are a man!" Then they glazed; he took a few faltering steps and fell down, uttering a cry so lamentable and full of anguish that I stood staring, dumb and horror-stricken, at his little corpse. He was buried in the garden under a white rose-tree which still marks his grave.

Theophile Gautier

One day, often with no forewarning whatever, he is gone from the house and never returns. He has felt the presaging shadow of death, and he goes to meet it in the old unchanging way of the wild—alone. A cat does not want to die with the smell of humanity in his nostrils and the noise of humanity in his delicate peaked ears.

Alan Devoe

I lost more than a cat: I lost an alarm clock.

Sylvia Kelly

Another cat? Perhaps. For love there is also a season; its seeds must be resown. But a family cat is not replaceable like a wornout coat or a set of tires. Each new kitten becomes its own cat, and none is repeated. I am four cats old, measuring out my life in friends that have succeeded but not replaced one another.

Irving Townsend

Dear little ghost, whose memory has never faded from my heart, accept this book, dedicated to thee, and to all thy cherished race. Sleep sweetly in the fields of asphodel, and waken, as of old, to stretch thy languid length, and purr thy soft contentment to the skies.

Agnes Repplier

Oh, Charles. Did we do you a disservice, to make you think that people were to be trusted after all? Did you lose your field smarts because of us? Did you think those men coming across the cornfield would stop to scratch you behind the ears? Was it a swift explosion of fur and flesh, only a momentary dazzle of pain? I hope so.

A. L. Hart

Heathcliff's death shocked my cats as much as it did me. Janine wept for the old faker and I confess I did the same. At my worktable, I sat alone—with the feeling of disagreeable lightness that comes when a cat just left your lap. Seeing his box in the corner, and a few tangled strings about the floor, I half expected Heathcliff himself to arrive at any moment. But, rationally, I knew I should never see my old friend again. For my remaining tigers, it was a more difficult matter. This time, I felt that the boundary between their world and mine had never been drawn so sharply. My cats could not ask me what had happened and it was impossible for me to tell them. They would somehow have to understand in their own way. I could not share the human faculty of resignation.

Lloyd Alexander

Alas, Grosvenor, to-day poor Rumpel was found dead, after as long and happy a life as cat could wish for, if cats form wishes on that subject. His full titles were: The Most Noble, the Archduke Rumpelstiltzchen, Marcus Macbum, Earl Tomlefnagne, Baron Raticide, Waowhler and Scratch. There should be a court-mourning in Catland...

Robert Southey

He was an elegant old gentleman, our Sam. In human years, he was about 133 and that should be enough to satisfy anybody. Anybody, that is, except a courageous cat who seemed almost human and two humans who married too late to start a family and settled for a pet.

Patty Cormaney

He purred when I stroked him. If he was really ill he was making no fuss or complaint. An hour later I carried him downstairs to give him his pill, and then I saw that he was worse. He lay listlessly in my arms, and the lightness of him frightened me. He seemed to have lost weight very suddenly.

I put him gently down on a cushion in front of the fire and he began to cough silently, his tongue hanging out. I hurried to get a kettle of boiling water for the friar's balsam. When I returned a few minutes later he was behind the curtains of the French windows. I picked him up and he lay still in my arms, his jaw sagging. As gently as I could I put him in his basket, which I had put on a chair over the steaming kettle. He rose feebly to his feet, turned round twice, and laid down as if to sleep. But I knew it was no ordinary sleep. My little cat was dead.

Michael Joseph

Unlike many cats, Puddy had always loved the wind. Even in a gale nothing had delighted him more than to rush out into it and stand, braced against it, letting the wind play over his fur and bend his whiskers backwards. Now for ten minutes, he remained, barely able to stand, letting the coolness play about him, feeling his fur ripple in the evening air.

That was the last wind Puddy was to know. Elva picked him up at length, and, looking at her gratefully with his one beautiful eye, Puddy let what seemed to be a great sigh pass through his whole body. We carried him inside, and he died shortly afterwards. We buried him in the rose-garden, where he had often slept in the shade of a tall photinia hedge.

Frank Legg

In the basement, where he followed me every morning while I exercised, I have decided not to clean up a small splotch of litter that spilled out of his box over in a corner— because it contains a perfect footprint.

Darryl Sifford

I discover her anew in each black cat I see. She is present in my joys and deepest sorrows, and reflected in the eyes of one who loves his cat. And sometimes, when a grayness falls upon an autumn day, or when the air is full of promises of rain, sometimes then I feel her near.

Samantha Mooney

Beginnings

Kittens, kittens, showers of kittens, visitations of kittens. So many, you see them as Kitten, like leaves growing on a bare branch, staying heavy and green, then falling exactly the same every year. People coming to visit say: What happened to that lovely kitten? What lovely kitten? They are all lovely kittens.

Doris Lessing

There is no more intrepid explorer than a kitten.

Champfleury

An ordinary kitten will ask more questions than any five-year-old boy.

Carl Van Vechten

I have just been given a very engaging Persian kitten...and his opinion is that I have been given to him.

Evelyn Underhill

Gather kittens while you may,
    Time brings only sorrow;
And the kittens of today
    Will be old cats tomorrow.

Oliver Herford

A kitten is the delight of a household. All day long a comedy is played by this incomparable actor.

Champfleury

Four little Persians, but one only looked in my direction. I extended a tentative finger and two soft paws clung to it. There was a contented sound of purring, I suspect on both our parts.

George Freedley

A kitten is so flexible that she is almost double; the hind parts are equivalent to another kitten with which the forepart plays. She does not discover that her tail belongs to her until you tread on it.

Henry David Thoreau

A kitten is the most irresistible comedian in the world. Its wide-open eyes gleam with wonder and mirth. It darts madly at nothing at all, and then, as though suddenly checked in the pursuit, prances sideways on its hind legs with ridiculous agility and zeal.

Agnes Repplier

A kitten is not a pretty thing at birth. For many days it is a wriggling mite of lumpy flesh and sinew, blind and unaware, making soft sucking noises with its wet, toothless mouth, and smelling of milk.

Alan Devoe

Everything that moves serves to amuse them. They believe that all nature is occupied with their diversion.

Moncriff

A kitten is more amusing than half the people one is obliged to live with.

Lady Sydney Morgan

Young kittens assume that all other animals are cats, approach them with jaunty friendliness, and invite them to play.

Muriel Beadle

A child is a person who can't understand why someone would give away a perfectly good kitten.

Doug Larson

A kitten is chiefly remarkable for rushing about like mad at nothing whatever, and generally stopping before it gets there.

Agnes Repplier

No matter how much cats fight, there always seem to be plenty of kittens.

Abraham Lincoln

A kitten is the rosebud in the garden of the animal kingdom.

Robert Southey

About the Author

C.E. Crimmins, humorist, writer, and slave to three felines, is the author of over a dozen books, including *Curse of the Mommy*; *When My Parents Were My Age, They Were Old*; and *The Seven Habits of Highly Defective People*. Her articles have appeared in *Redbook*, *Success*, *Savvy*, *Working Woman*, *Parents Digest*, and *Funny Times*. She lives in Philadelphia and is still waiting for her cats to say something quotable.